TAM KERR
THE HOME RENOVATION DIARY

AUSTIN MACAULEY PUBLISHERS™
LONDON * CAMBRIDGE * NEW YORK * SHARJAH

A CIP catalogue record for this title is available from the British Library.

ISBN 9781788781183 (Paperback)
ISBN 9781788781190 (Hardback)
ISBN 9781788781206 (E-Book)
www.austinmacauley.com

First Published (2018)
Austin Macauley Publishers ™ Ltd
25 Canada Square
Canary Wharf
London
E14 5LQ

AN EASY TO USE JOURNAL
IN WHICH TO KEEP VITAL
INFORMATION RELATING TO
HOMES AND RENOVATIONS

USE TO RECORD DETAILS OF
- THE PROPERTY
- PURCHASE/FINANCE
- PLANNING APPLICATIONS
- APPROVALS/REJECTIONS
- TRADESPEOPLE/OTHERS
- QUOTES/COSTS/BUDGETS
- SCHEDULES/DEADLINES
- MATERIALS/FITTINGS
- AND MUCH MORE

THE HOME RENOVATION DIARY

A MUST HAVE PUBLICATION FOR HOME OWNERS, RENOVATORS, BUILDERS AND TRADESPEOPLE

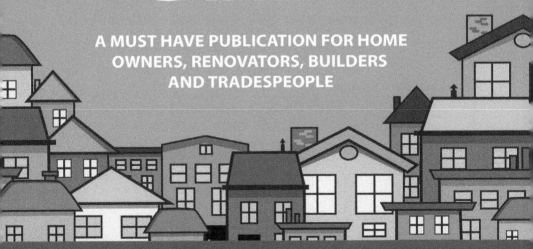

WRITTEN AND COMPILED BY TAM KERR
FORMER BUILDING EDITOR WITH BETTER HOMES & GARDENS MAGAZINE (AUSTRALIA)

THE IMPORTANCE OF KEEPING THIS HOME RENOVATION DIARY

When renovating or building it is vital to keep an accurate record of every detail relating to the project.

Not knowing precisely what has been discussed, decided or planned, or what has been done or spent, can easily lead to confusion, disruption, disputation, delays and increased costs.

The Home Renovation Diary prevents such problems by giving those involved in home renovation or building projects immediate access to vital information about the job, people engaged in it, schedules, budgets, expenditures, materials, fittings, appliances and more.

Often, important communications between home owners or renovators and their builders, tradespeople, suppliers and others are done verbally or through scribbled notes. Such practices can lead to costly misunderstandings, mistakes and delays.

The Home Renovation Diary prevents this from happening and ensures a smooth and faster operation with maximum success and minimum frustration.

It also provides quick and easy access to complete expenditure details should such be required for selling, business or taxation purposes.

ABOUT THE AUTHOR

The Home Renovation Diary has been written and compiled by Tam Kerr, former Building Editor with Better Homes and Gardens Magazine (Australia).

Tam has renovated a number of properties and supervised the total build of another. On every occasion, he worked closely with architects and designers as well as local authorities and planners. Liaising regularly with tradespeople and suppliers was a vital part of the success of all of the projects.

2 /

NDEX

MANY VALUABLE TIPS FOR
RENOVATORS CAN ALSO BE
FOUND THROUGHOUT
THE DIARY

/3

GENERAL INFORMATION

PROPERTY DETAILS

Address _____

_____

Type of Building _____

Area size _____

Construction _____

Zoning _____

Date Built _____

Lounges _____

Bedrooms _____

Kitchen _____

Bathrooms _____

Laundry _____

Garage _____

Car Port _____

Heating Type _____

Garden Size/Description _____

_____

Garden Walls/Fencing _____

——— HANDY TIP ———

Insurance Coverage: Check to see if you should take out insurance to cover the project and those working on it. Some tradespeople and others engaged in the work will have their own insurance which you should check, but others may not. And, if someone is involved in a serious accident and does not have personal insurance, you could be held liable and sued.

GENERAL INFORMATION

PROPERTY INSURANCE

Company _____

Representative _____

Address _____

_____

Phone _____ Fax _____

Email _____

Type of Coverage _____

_____

Period of Cover _____

Payout Value _____

Annual Payment _____

Periodic Payments _____

HANDY TIP

Safety First: When purchasing a property, particularly if it is old, and before doing any work on it, have the building professionally inspected to make sure it is structurally sound, water proof and safe. This would most probably have to be done as a condition of receiving a loan. But, if you do not require a loan, or you are about to renovate a property you already own, it is still worth having such checks done. They could save you a lot of grief and cost in the future. A qualified or licensed electrician and plumber should also be engaged at the outset to check all of the wiring and electrics, as well as the plumbing and drainage.

5 /

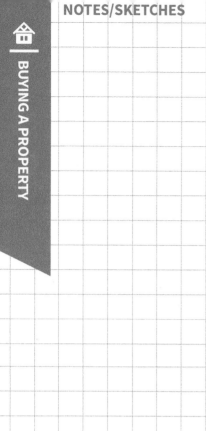

GENERAL INFORMATION

BUYING A PROPERTY

VENDOR

Name _____

Address _____

_____

Phone _____ Fax _____

Email _____

Real Estate Company _____

Representative _____

Address _____

_____

Phone _____ Fax _____

Email _____

PURCHASER

Name _____

Address _____

_____

Phone _____ Fax _____

Email _____

Contract Details _____

_____

Price Sought _____ Price Paid _____

Amount of Loan (if applicable) _____

Type of Loan _____ Period of Loan _____

Repayment Details _____

Lender _____

Representative _____

Address _____

_____

Phone _____ Fax _____

Email _____

LEGAL REPRESENTATIVES

VENDOR'S LEGAL REPRESENTATIVE

Name _____

Company _____

Address _____

_____

Phone _____ Fax _____

Email _____

Date Sales Contract Signed _____

Date Transfer Registered _____

Date of Occupancy _____

Costs _____

_____

Dates and Details of Meetings _____

_____

_____

PURCHASER'S LEGAL REPRESENTATIVE

Name _____

Company _____

Address _____

_____

Phone _____ Fax _____

Email _____

Date Sales Contract Signed _____

Date Transfer Registered _____

Date of Occupancy _____

Costs _____

Dates and Details of Meetings _____

7 /

GENERAL INFORMATION

PLANS

ARCHITECT, DRAFTSMAN, DESIGNER

Name _____

Company _____

Address _____

_____

Phone _____ Fax _____

Email _____

Contract Details _____

_____

_____

_____

_____

Proposed Cost of Plans _____

Actual Cost _____

Variation _____

Date of Completion _____

Dates and Details of Meetings _____

_____

——— *HANDY TIP* ———

Be Available To Meet Officials: Depending on the extent of the work you are doing, it might be necessary for building and other officials to visit the site. So, arrange a time and make sure you are there, along with your builder if you have one, to discuss the project. It is much better to discuss any concerns and resolve them onsite as soon as possible.

GENERAL INFORMATION

LODGEMENT OF PLANS

COUNCIL OR LOCAL AUTHORITY

Name _____

Address _____

_____

Phone _____ Fax _____

Email _____

Date of Lodgment of Plans _____

Dates of Inspections _____

Inspector's Name _____

Phone _____ Fax _____

Email _____

Points from Inspections _____

_____

_____

_____

_____

Date of Final Approval _____

Costs and Charges _____

Budget _____

Variation _____

_____

_____

_____

9 /

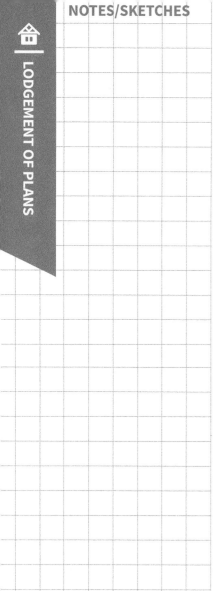

LODGEMENT OF PLANS

LODGEMENT OF PLANS

WATER BOARD OR LOCAL AUTHORITY

Name _____

Address _____

_____

Phone _____ Fax _____

Email _____

Date of Lodgement of Plans _____

Dates of Inspections _____

Inspector's Name _____

Phone _____ Fax _____

Email _____

Points from Inspections _____

_____

_____

_____

Date of Final Approval _____

Costs and Charges _____

Budget _____

Variation _____

_____

———— *HANDY TIP* ————

Council Safety Requirements: If the work is
major and outside, councils or local authorities will
most likely insist on having the area suitably fenced
off with appropriate signage displayed. Check with
them to see if that is a requirement for your project.

BUILDER

BUILDER

Name _____

Company _____

Address _____

_____

Phone _____ Fax _____

Email _____

Licence _____

Insurance _____

Job Description _____

_____

_____

_____

_____

Materials _____

_____

_____

Starting Date _____

Scheduled Completion Date _____

Completion Date _____

Quoted Price _____

Actual Price _____

Variation _____

Budget _____

Variation _____

PLUMBER

Name _____

Company _____

Address _____

_____

Phone _____ Fax _____

Email _____

Licence _____

Insurance _____

Job Description _____

_____

_____

_____

_____

Materials _____

_____

_____

Starting Date _____

Scheduled Completion Date _____

Completion Date _____

Quoted Price _____

Actual Price _____

Variation _____

Budget _____

Variation _____

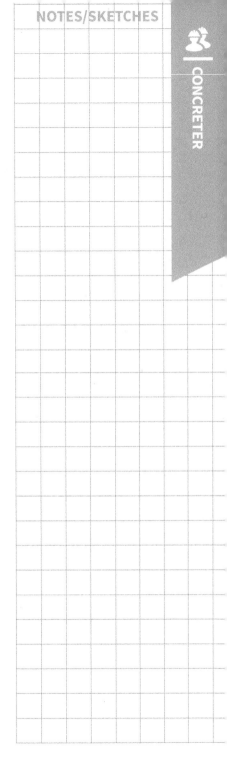

TRADESPEOPLE

CONCRETER

Name _____

Company _____

Address _____

_____

Phone _____ Fax _____

Email _____

Licence _____

Insurance _____

Job Description _____

_____

_____

_____

_____

Materials _____

_____

_____

Starting Date _____

Scheduled Completion Date _____

Completion Date _____

Quoted Price _____

Actual Price _____

Variation _____

Budget _____

Variation _____

BRICKLAYER

BRICKLAYER

Name _____

Company _____

Address _____

_____

Phone _____ Fax _____

Email _____

Licence _____

Insurance _____

Job Description _____

_____

_____

_____

_____

Materials _____

_____

_____

Starting Date _____

Scheduled Completion Date _____

Completion Date _____

Quoted Price _____

Actual Price _____

Variation _____

Budget _____

Variation _____

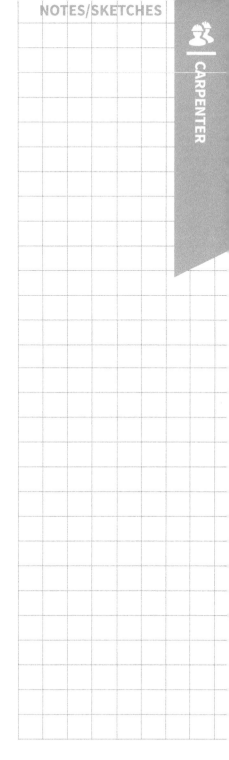

TRADESPEOPLE

CARPENTER

Name _____

Company _____

Address _____

_____

Phone _____ Fax _____

Email _____

Licence _____

Insurance _____

Job Description _____

_____

_____

_____

_____

Materials _____

_____

_____

Starting Date _____

Scheduled Completion Date _____

Completion Date _____

Quoted Price _____

Actual Price _____

Variation _____

Budget _____

Variation _____

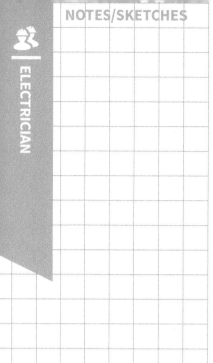

NOTES/SKETCHES

TRADESPEOPLE

ELECTRICIAN

Name _____

Company _____

Address _____

_____

Phone _____ Fax _____

Email _____

Licence _____

Insurance _____

Job Description _____

_____

_____

_____

_____

Materials _____

_____

_____

Starting Date _____

Scheduled Completion Date _____

Completion Date _____

Quoted Price _____

Actual Price _____

Variation _____

Budget _____

Variation _____

TILER

TRADESPEOPLE

TILER

Name _____

Company _____

Address _____

_____

Phone _____ Fax _____

Email _____

Licence _____

Insurance _____

Job Description _____

_____

_____

_____

_____

Materials _____

_____

_____

Starting Date _____

Scheduled Completion Date _____

Completion Date _____

Quoted Price _____

Actual Price _____

Variation _____

Budget _____

Variation _____

PLASTERER

PLASTERER

Name _____

Company _____

Address _____

_____

Phone _____ Fax _____

Email _____

Licence _____

Insurance _____

Job Description _____

_____

_____

_____

_____

Materials _____

_____

_____

Starting Date _____

Scheduled Completion Date _____

Completion Date _____

Quoted Price _____

Actual Price _____

Variation _____

Budget _____

Variation _____

TRADESPEOPLE
—

PAINTER

Name _____

Company _____

Address _____

_____

Phone _____ Fax _____

Email _____

Licence _____

Insurance _____

Job Description _____

_____

_____

_____

_____

Materials _____

_____

_____

Starting Date _____

Scheduled Completion Date _____

Completion Date _____

Quoted Price _____

Actual Price _____

Variation _____

Budget _____

Variation _____

CARPET/FLOOR LAYER

TRADESPEOPLE

CARPET/FLOOR LAYER

Name _____

Company _____

Address _____

_____

Phone _____ Fax _____

Email _____

Licence _____

Insurance _____

Job Description _____

_____

_____

_____

_____

Materials _____

_____

_____

Starting Date _____

Scheduled Completion Date _____

Completion Date _____

Quoted Price _____

Actual Price _____

Variation _____

Budget _____

Variation _____

TRADESPEOPLE

AIR CONDITIONING INSTALLER

Name _____

Company _____

Address _____

_____

Phone _____ Fax _____

Email _____

Licence _____

Insurance _____

Job Description _____

_____

Brand/Model _____

_____

_____

Starting Date _____

Scheduled Completion Date _____

Completion Date _____

Quoted Price _____

Actual Price _____

Variation _____

Budget _____

Variation _____

/ 21

TRADESPEOPLE

FENCER

Name _____

Company _____

Address _____

_____

Phone _____ Fax _____

Email _____

Licence _____

Insurance _____

Job Description _____

_____

_____

_____

_____

Materials _____

_____

_____

Starting Date _____

Scheduled Completion Date _____

Completion Date _____

Quoted Price _____

Actual Price _____

Variation _____

Budget _____

Variation _____

TRADESPEOPLE

GARDENER/LANDSCAPER

Name _____

Company _____

Address _____

_____

Phone _____ Fax _____

Email _____

Licence _____

Insurance _____

Job Description _____

_____

_____

_____

_____

Materials _____

_____

_____

Starting Date _____

Scheduled Completion Date _____

Completion Date _____

Quoted Price _____

Actual Price _____

Variation _____

Budget _____

Variation _____

/ 23

MATERIALS

BRICKS

Types/Colours/Quantities _____

_____

_____

_____

_____

Cost _____

Budget _____

Variation _____

Scheduled Delivery Date _____

Delivery Date _____

Supplier _____

_____

Address _____

_____

Phone _____ Fax _____

Email _____

HANDY TIP

Don't Overload Your Vehicle: Be careful not to overload your car with too much weight. The last thing you want is to damage the vehicle. So, organise alternative ways of having heavy materials and items delivered.

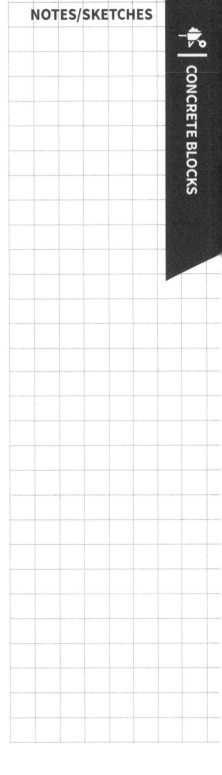

CONCRETE BLOCKS

MATERIALS

CONCRETE BLOCKS

Types/Colours/Quantities _____

_____

_____

_____

_____

Cost _____

Budget _____

Variation _____

Scheduled Delivery Date _____

Delivery Date _____

Supplier _____

_____

Address _____

_____

Phone _____ Fax _____

Email _____

HANDY TIP

Check Ground is Solid: If you are planning to have large concrete trucks or heavy loads of bricks or other materials delivered on to the site, make sure the ground is solid and level enough to take their weight.

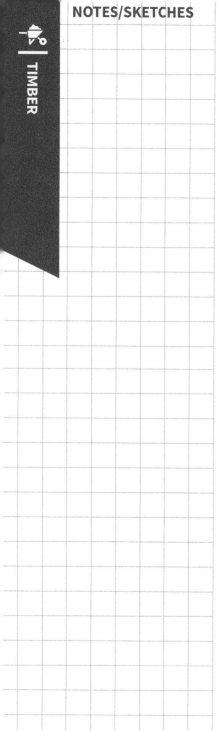

MATERIALS

TIMBER

Types/Colours/Quantities _____

_____

_____

_____

_____

Cost _____

Budget _____

Variation _____

Scheduled Delivery Date _____

Delivery Date _____

Supplier _____

_____

Address _____

_____

Phone _____ Fax _____

Email _____

——— *HANDY TIP* ———

Leave Space for Vehicles: If you are doing major renovations or construction, you will probably need to have large quantities of materials delivered. So make sure the delivery trucks have suitable access to the site.

MATERIALS

PLASTERBOARD/ WALL LININGS

Types/Colours/Quantities _____

_____

_____

_____

_____

Cost _____

Budget _____

Variation _____

Scheduled Delivery Date _____

Delivery Date _____

Supplier _____

_____

Address _____

_____

Phone _____ Fax _____

Email _____

HANDY TIP

Be Wary of Large Vehicles: Often trucks and other commercial vehicles have to reverse so be there or have someone else available to guide them from behind. Again, keep children well out of the way.

/ 27

CORNICES

MATERIALS

CORNICES

Types/Colours/Quantities _____

_____

_____

_____

_____

Cost _____

Budget _____

Variation _____

Scheduled Delivery Date _____

Delivery Date _____

Supplier _____

_____

Address _____

_____

Phone _____ Fax _____

Email _____

———— *HANDY TIP* ————

Allow for Weather: Research thoroughly
what weather you can expect each day. As well as
checking newspapers and local radio or television
stations, you can also use Google to find long term
forecasts. You can then use that information to plan
your work and delivery schedules.

MATERIALS

TILES

LOUNGE FLOORS

Types/Colours/Quantities _____

_____

_____

_____

Total Area _____

Cost _____

Budget _____

Variation _____

Scheduled Delivery Date _____

Delivery Date _____

Supplier _____

_____

Address _____

_____

Phone _____ Fax _____

Email _____

--- ***HANDY TIP*** ---

You Don't Have To Tile: If you want to quickly
and relatively inexpensively change the appearance
of the kitchen, bathroom/toilet and other areas,
consider painting the tiles. These days, there are
paints on the market especially made for use on
tiles. Get advice from your local paint supplier.
Renewing the taps is another easy way of freshening
up some areas.

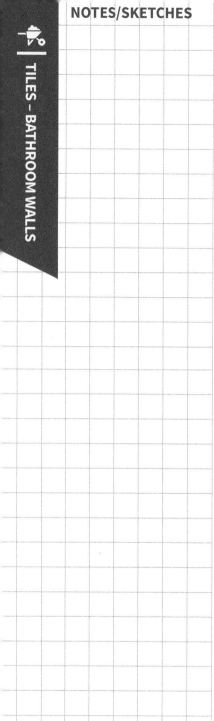

MATERIALS

TILES

BATHROOM FLOORS

Types/Colours/Quantities _____
_____
_____
_____

Total Area _____

Cost _____

Budget _____

Variation _____

Scheduled Delivery Date _____

Delivery Date _____

Supplier _____
_____

Address _____
_____

Phone _____ Fax _____

Email _____

─────────── **HANDY TIP** ───────────

Free Deliveries: You might find that local
hardware, paint or building suppliers will deliver or
provide the loan of a trailer free if you purchase a
large amount. So when making your purchases,
ask them.

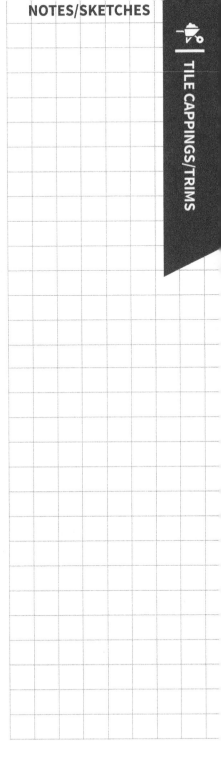

MATERIALS

TILE CAPPINGS/TRIMS

BATHROOM WALLS

Types/Colours/Quantities _____

_____

_____

_____

Cost _____

Budget _____

Variation _____

Scheduled Delivery Date _____

Delivery Date _____

Supplier _____

_____

Address _____

_____

Phone _____ Fax _____

Email _____

HANDY TIP

Protect Materials and Equipment: If
you have to store materials and equipment or
appliances outside, cover them with tarpaulins or
plastic sheeting to protect them from the weather.

/ 31

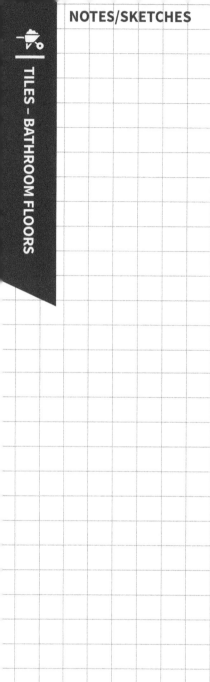

MATERIALS

TILES

BATHROOM FLOORS

Types/Colours/Quantities _____

_____

_____

_____

Total Area _____

Cost _____

Budget _____

Variation _____

Scheduled Delivery Date _____

Delivery Date _____

Supplier _____

_____

Address _____

_____

Phone _____ Fax _____

Email _____

HANDY TIP

Rubbish Removal: If you are undertaking major renovations, it is worthwhile hiring a 'skip' or trailer to remove the rubble and waste. Check around for the best prices. Skips are large, heavy bins and companies need to deliver them with special trucks and pick them up when full. If you are removing waste yourself, check with the local dumps to make sure they will accept the type of rubbish you will be bringing.

MATERIALS

TILES

KITCHEN WALLS

Types/Colours/Quantities _____

_____

_____

_____

Total Area _____

Cost _____

Budget _____

Variation _____

Scheduled Delivery Date _____

Delivery Date _____

Supplier _____

_____

Address _____

_____

Phone _____ Fax _____

Email _____

─── *HANDY TIP* ───

Rubbish or Treasure: When demolishing or
removing items or parts of the property, keep a look
out for anything you can use or sell. It is amazing
what others are willing to buy. What's the old saying?
'One man's rubbish is another man's treasure'.

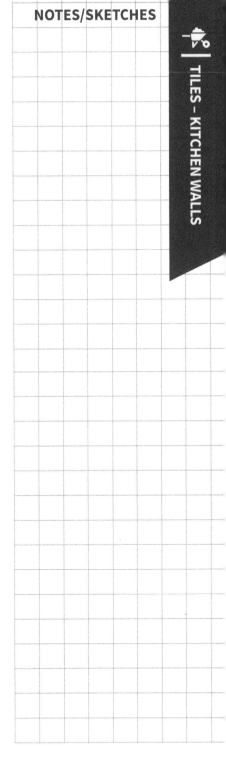

/ 33

MATERIALS

TILE CAPPINGS/TRIMS

KITCHEN WALLS

Types/Colours/Quantities _____

_____

_____

_____

Cost _____

Budget _____

Variation _____

Scheduled Delivery Date _____

Delivery Date _____

Supplier _____

_____

Address _____

_____

Phone _____ Fax _____

Email _____

HANDY TIP

Secure Your Property: During renovation or building, make sure your property is secured when no one is there. Tools are best taken with you if they cannot be secured on the premises. A property undergoing renovation or a building site seems to send out an open invitation to thieves and vandals. So, use whatever measures you need to keep it secure. Ways range from a padlocked gate to regular patrols by security companies.

MATERIALS

TILES

KITCHEN FLOOR

Types/Colours/Quantities _____

_____

_____

_____

Total Area _____

Cost _____

Budget _____

Variation _____

Scheduled Delivery Date _____

Delivery Date _____

Supplier _____

_____

Address _____

_____

Phone _____ Fax _____

Email _____

HANDY TIP

Keep Neighbours Onside: If you are planning major work, it is a good idea to keep neighbours who might be affected well informed. Getting them onside at the outset is much better than starting the work and having an annoyed or disgruntled neighbour coming to your door and complaining. They could even lodge complaints with the local council or authority. At your initial meeting with them, emphasize how you will do your best to keep any noise or disturbance to a minimum and have the work completed as quickly as possible. Also, point out how the improvements you will be making will help lift the value of all of the properties in the area.

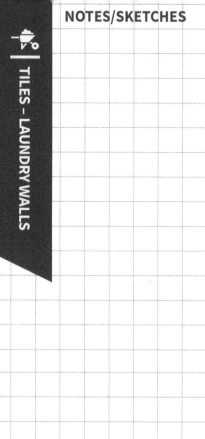

TILES – LAUNDRY WALLS

TILES

LAUNDRY WALLS

Types/Colours/Quantities _____

_____

_____

_____

Cost _____

Budget _____

Variation _____

Scheduled Delivery Date _____

Delivery Date _____

Supplier _____

_____

Address _____

_____

Phone _____ Fax _____

Email _____

HANDY TIP

First Aid: It is not uncommon for accidents to occur on renovation or building sites. So, have a first aid kit on hand in case of such emergencies. A simple first aid sheet or guide would also be handy. You should also have the number of the Ambulance readily available in case there has been a major accident.

MATERIALS

TILE CAPPINGS/TRIMS

LAUNDRY WALLS

Types/Colours/Quantities _____

_____

_____

_____

Cost _____

Budget _____

Variation _____

Scheduled Delivery Date _____

Delivery Date _____

Supplier _____

_____

Address _____

_____

Phone _____ Fax _____

Email _____

HANDY TIP

Children and Animals: By nature, children are tremendously curious which is wonderful. But on renovation or building sites, it can lead them into all sorts of trouble. Sure, take little Johnny and Mary onto the area to have a look at things, but keep them supervised at all times. Pets should never be allowed on renovation or building sites.

TILES – LAUNDRY FLOOR

MATERIALS

TILES

LAUNDRY FLOOR

Types/Colours/Quantities _____

_____

_____

_____

Total Area _____

Cost _____

Budget _____

Variation _____

Scheduled Delivery Date _____

Delivery Date _____

Supplier _____

_____

Address _____

_____

Phone _____ Fax _____

Email _____

——— HANDY TIP ———

Make Sure There is Water: Often, on building sites or when major renovation work is being carried out, the water supply has to be cut off. So, have fresh water available in appropriate containers.

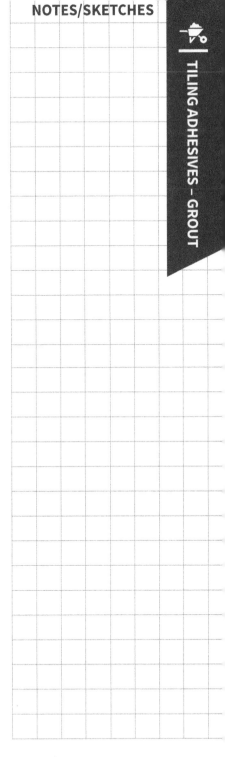

MATERIALS

TILING ADHESIVES

Types/Colours/Quantities _____

_____

_____

Scheduled Delivery Date _____

Delivery Date _____

Supplier _____

_____

Address _____

_____

Phone _____ Fax _____

Email _____

MATERIALS

GROUT

Types/Colours/Quantities _____

_____

_____

Scheduled Delivery Date _____

Delivery Date _____

Supplier _____

_____

Address _____

_____

Phone _____ Fax _____

Email _____

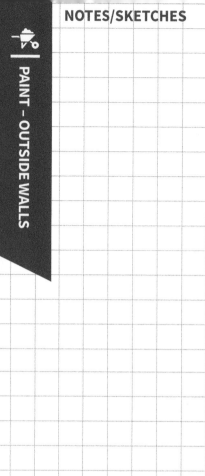

MATERIALS

PAINT

OUTSIDE WALLS

Types/Colours/Quantities _____

_____

_____

_____

Total Area _____

Cost _____

Budget _____

Variation _____

Scheduled Delivery Date _____

Delivery Date _____

Supplier _____

_____

Address _____

_____

Phone _____ Fax _____

Email _____

HANDY TIP

The Importance of Preparation: If you watch good tradespeople work, you will see they pay a lot of attention and time to preparation. Painters are a prime example. They will make sure the surfaces are perfect before painting. They will also use an appropriate primer or undercoat before applying the finishing paint or varnish. Even using the right type of sandpaper is important. Again, consult with the experts at your paint or hardware store.

MATERIALS

PAINT

OUTSIDE DOORS/WINDOWS

Types/Colours/Quantities _____

_____

_____

_____

Total Area _____

Cost _____

Budget _____

Variation _____

Scheduled Delivery Date _____

Delivery Date _____

Supplier _____

_____

Address _____

_____

Phone _____ Fax _____

Email _____

HANDY TIP

Choose The Correct Paint: Paint comes in a tremendous variety of colours. There are also many types for different applications. For instance, it would be totally inappropriate to use ceiling paint on floors which need hard wearing cover or outside which requires weather resistant paint. There are also paints which are made especially for 'wet' areas such as bathrooms. So, as with so many decisions, talk to the experts at your local supply company.

/ 41

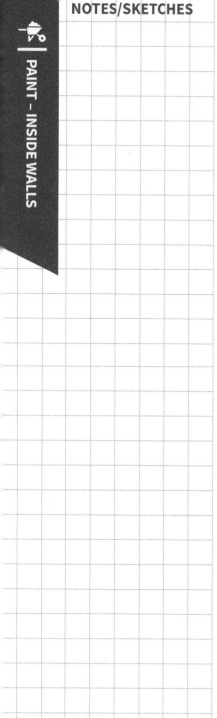

MATERIALS

PAINT

INSIDE WALLS

Types/Colours/Quantities _____

_____

_____

_____

Total Area _____

Cost _____

Budget _____

Variation _____

Scheduled Delivery Date _____

Delivery Date _____

Supplier _____

_____

Address _____

_____

Phone _____ Fax _____

Email _____

HANDY TIP

Paint Brushes/Rollers: Paint brushes come in all shapes and sizes. They also vary greatly in quality and price. Using a good quality paint brush will make the job easier and look more professional. However, if you are painting something less obvious such as an out of the way wall, you might use cheaper brushes. Different roller covers are designed for different surfaces. Again, your paint supplier will be able to advise you.

MATERIALS

PAINT

INSIDE DOORS

Types/Colours/Quantities _____

_____

_____

_____

Total Area _____

Cost _____

Budget _____

Variation _____

Scheduled Delivery Date _____

Delivery Date _____

Supplier _____

_____

Address _____

_____

Phone _____ Fax _____

Email _____

HANDY TIP

Purchasing Materials: Tradespeople will sometimes purchase materials for your job themselves. But if you have to do it, see if you can get a discount by purchasing through your tradepersons' account. It is also possible you can get a trade or home renovators' discount. You might also save by paying cash. Sometimes, savings can be made by purchasing materials and fittings from renovation or second hand building material shops and yards. These are particularly worthwhile checking if the renovation involves a classical period house or unit, or if you are looking for something a bit more offbeat or funky. Tradespeople and others you have engaged should also be able to advise you on the best places to source materials.

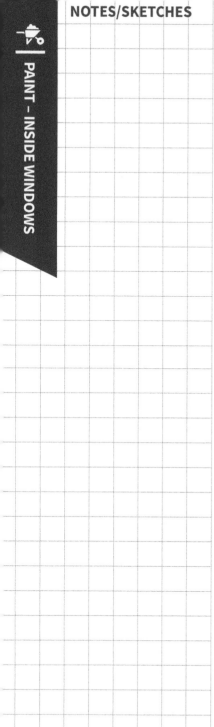

PAINT – INSIDE WINDOWS

PAINT

INSIDE WINDOWS/SKIRTINGS

Types/Colours/Quantities _____

_____

_____

_____

Total Area _____

Cost _____

Budget _____

Variation _____

Scheduled Delivery Date _____

Delivery Date _____

Supplier _____

_____

Address _____

_____

Phone _____ Fax _____

Email _____

HANDY TIP

Use Ladders Safely: One of the most frequently used pieces of equipment in renovations and building are extension and step-ladders. Check them before use to make sure they are in good working condition. When using extension ladders, keep them well away from overhead power lines and electricity boxes. Make sure any ladders you are using are firmly placed on the surface. You can use a good size piece of timber under one leg to level them off. Sometimes, it is worthwhile having someone hold the ladders steady when you are on them.

FENCING

TIMBER PALINGS

Style/Size/Quantities _____

_____

_____

_____

Cost _____

Budget _____

Variation _____

Scheduled Delivery Date _____

Delivery Date _____

Supplier _____

_____

Address _____

_____

Phone _____ Fax _____

Email _____

HANDY TIP

Appropriate Tools: You can spend a lot of money on tools. Every hardware store offers a wide range of electric and manual tools. A good quality battery operated drill is a tool that, after the renovations, you will most likely find very useful to have around. Choose one which has a lot of power and comes with two batteries. Also, buy good quality drills which come individually or in boxed sets. Unless you have to cut a lot of timber or wood sheeting, a good quality hand saw is most likely all you'll need. Ask your hardware salesperson to advise you on the most suitable tools to buy for the work you will be doing.

FENCING

TIMBER FENCE POSTS

Style/Size/Quantities _____

_____

_____

_____

Cost _____

Budget _____

Variation _____

Scheduled Delivery Date _____

Delivery Date _____

Supplier _____

_____

Address _____

_____

Phone _____ Fax _____

Email _____

HANDY TIP

Hiring Tools and Equipment: You might come across jobs which require specialist tools and equipment. Large ladders or paint sprays, for instance, are things which you might only need once. So, visit your local equipment hire store and check out what they have available. You'll be amazed at the range of equipment they will have in stock. Some hardware stores also hire out equipment and tools. Alternately, you might have a relative or friend who has something you can borrow.

FENCING

TIMBER FENCE CROSS RAILS/SPARS

Style/Size/Quantities _____

_____

_____

_____

Cost _____

Budget _____

Variation _____

Scheduled Delivery Date _____

Delivery Date _____

Supplier _____

_____

Address _____

_____

Phone _____ Fax _____

Email _____

HANDY TIP

Call On Family and Friends: A very effective way to cut back on costs is to ask for help from family and friends. There are a great many time consuming and simple jobs on a renovation or building site that can be done. They range from clearing rubbish and taking it to the tip to going to get items and materials from the hardware store or other places. You might find that not everyone will want to help, but there is no harm in asking.

FENCING

FENCE NAILS/ ATTACHMENTS

Style/Size/Quantities _____

_____

_____

_____

Cost _____

Budget _____

Variation _____

Scheduled Delivery Date _____

Delivery Date _____

Supplier _____

_____

Address _____

_____

Phone _____ Fax _____

Email _____

HANDY TIP

Nailing Tips: When nailing, use the appropriate hammer. A 'claw' hammer is the one favoured by most tradespeople. The 'claw' part is used to pull out nails. To protect the surface from damage when doing this, place a piece of timber under the hammer head. You can also use a piece of wood if the nail is sticking far out. If you are worried about causing damage to the surface when hammering, hold a piece of timber or other suitable material alongside the nail. Also, if you are using very small nails, use a pair of 'narrow-nose' pliers to hold the nail when hitting it.

FENCING

POST STIRRUPS/ GROUND ATTACHMENTS

Style/Size/Quantities _____

_____

_____

_____

Cost _____

Budget _____

Variation _____

Scheduled Delivery Date _____

Delivery Date _____

Supplier _____

_____

Address _____

_____

Phone _____ Fax _____

Email _____

HANDY TIP

Get Young Help: Most young people are happy to earn extra cash these days. So, if there are any teenagers you know of – perhaps sons and daughters of relatives or friends, or neighbours – see if they would be willing to give you a hand. There are plenty of simple, and very importantly, SAFE jobs, which they could do. You should always get their parents' approval before engaging them. What to pay them? Well, you could be guided by how much the local McDonalds store pays its young employees.

FENCING

FENCING OTHER THAN TIMBER

Types/Specification/Number of Sections/Fittings _____

_____

_____

_____

_____

_____

Total Area _____

Cost _____

Budget _____

Variation _____

Scheduled Delivery Date _____

Delivery Date _____

Supplier _____

_____

Address _____

_____

Phone _____ Fax _____

Email _____

HANDY TIP

Clear Working Space: If you are doing major work in a particular room or area, move all, or most of what is in there, out. And to protect the floor, lay down 'drop sheets'. Having a clear space to work will make the job so much easier, particularly if you need to use ladders.

FENCING

CONCRETE FOR POSTS/STIRRUPS

Amount _____

_____

_____

_____

Cost _____

Budget _____

Variation _____

Scheduled Delivery Date _____

Delivery Date _____

Supplier _____

_____

Address _____

_____

Phone _____ Fax _____

Email _____

HANDY TIP

The Correct Fasteners: There are a massive amount of fasteners on the market. And they are all designed to do specific jobs. Often, you have a choice of more than one to do the same task. Walls, for instance, are made of a great variety of materials and certain fasteners are made for some walls and not others. Again, talk to your expert hardware store staff and get their guidance.

/ 51

GARDEN

LANDSCAPER/GARDENER/ COMPANY

Name _____

Company _____

Address _____

_____

Phone _____ Fax _____

Email _____

Licence _____

Insurance _____

Work contracted for _____

_____

Materials Supplied by Landscaper _____

_____

Starting Date _____

Scheduled Completion Date _____

Actual Completion Date _____

Variation _____

Quoted Price _____

Actual Price _____

Variation _____

Budget _____

Variation _____

GARDEN

LANDSCAPING

GROUND COVER/MATERIALS

Types/Amount/Number _____

_____

_____

_____

_____

Total Area _____

Cost _____

Budget _____

Variation _____

Scheduled Delivery Date _____

Delivery Date _____

Supplier _____

_____

Address _____

_____

Phone _____ Fax _____

Email _____

HANDY TIP

Make Sure Everyone Understands: When dealing with anyone, be they government officials or tradespeople and suppliers, make sure everyone is absolutely clear about what has been decided. Mistakes cost money and time and should be avoided at all costs.

GARDEN

LANDSCAPING

PAVERS

Styles/Colours/Quantities/Cost _____

_____

_____

_____

Total Area _____

Cost _____

Budget _____

Variation _____

Scheduled Delivery Date _____

Delivery Date _____

Supplier _____

_____

Address _____

_____

Phone _____ Fax _____

Email _____

———————— HANDY TIP ————————

A Simple Shelf/Seat: If you need a shelf or shelves in the garden, shed, garage or elsewhere, one of the easiest and least expensive ways to build one is to purchase from your local hardware store or building supplier depot, one or more treated pine sleepers and the appropriate number of concrete building blocks. The numbers depend on the height and size of the shelf. Simply place one or more blocks apart at the end of the sleeper/s or shortened lengths and place the timber on top. To build one or more shelves, place one or more blocks on the end of the first shelf and so on. Make sure you only build to a safe level. The same method can be applied if you want a garden seat. The finishing touch is a coat of paint.

GARDEN

LANDSCAPING

CONCRETE

Type/Amount _____

_____

_____

_____

Total Area _____

Cost _____

Budget _____

Variation _____

Scheduled Delivery Date _____

Delivery Date _____

Supplier _____

_____

Address _____

_____

Phone _____ Fax _____

Email _____

_____ **HANDY TIP** _____

Don't Overdo It: Many of us become so caught up and eager watching the work progress, we can overdo it. Don't tackle something which might well be beyond your capabilities. Also, if you are overly tired or exhausted, you could well become a liability to yourself and others. Getting injured can cause all sorts of problems and even set back the project. So, recognize when you need help and get it.

GARDEN

LANDSCAPING

EDGING

Types/Quantities/Dates of Planting _____

_____

_____

_____

Cost _____

Budget _____

Variation _____

Scheduled Delivery Date _____

Delivery Date _____

Supplier _____

_____

Address _____

_____

Phone _____ Fax _____

Email _____

——— HANDY TIP ———

Use Drawings and Sketches: Keep a clipboard
and pen on hand so that when you are discussing
various matters with tradespeople and others, you
can illustrate what you are referring to.

GARDEN

LANDSCAPING

GRASS

Types/Amount _____

_____

_____

_____

Total Area _____

Cost _____

Budget _____

Variation _____

Scheduled Delivery Date _____

Delivery Date _____

Supplier _____

_____

Address _____

_____

Phone _____ Fax _____

Email _____

HANDY TIP

Nine-To-Five is Not An Option: While those you employ on the project might be able to work to a certain time frame, you should expect to do more. The longer you apply yourself to the job, the quicker it will be finished.

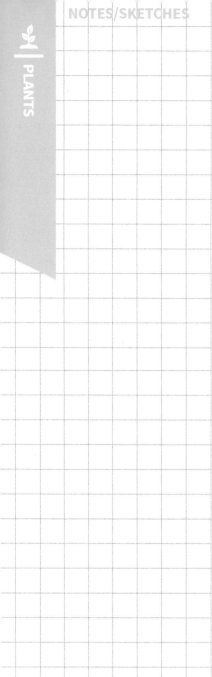

GARDEN

LANDSCAPING

PLANTS

Types/Quantities _____

_____

_____

_____

Cost _____

Budget _____

Variation _____

Scheduled Delivery Date _____

Delivery Date _____

Supplier _____

_____

Address _____

_____

Phone _____ Fax _____

Email _____

HANDY TIP

Fire Hazards: During major renovations and building, there can be many fire hazards. An obvious one is flammable liquids used in painting and cleaning. So, be aware of that and store them in safe, cool (don't leave in the hot sun) places. Other fire hazards include rubbish which a carelessly discarded cigarette can quickly ignite. Faulty electric wiring has also been known to cause fires. So, be constantly aware of the risks of fire. You might want to keep a fire extinguisher or fire blanket handy.

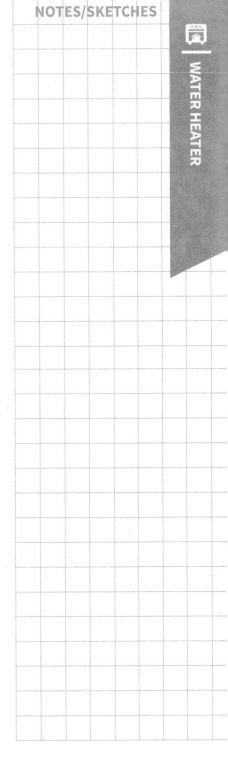

APPLIANCES – FITTINGS

WATER HEATER

Type/Size/Brand _____

_____

_____

_____

Warranty _____

Cost _____

Budget _____

Variation _____

Scheduled Delivery Date _____

Delivery Date _____

Variation _____

Supplier _____

_____

Address _____

_____

Phone _____ Fax _____

Email _____

HANDY TIP

Shop Around and Bargain: When buying virtually anything these days, it can be well worth your while bargaining with suppliers. Substantial savings can be made by comparing prices and discussing a deal. This can prove extremely worthwhile when purchasing large quantities of materials as well as kitchen, laundry and other appliances.

STOVE/COOKER

STOVE/COOKER

Type/Size/Brand/Colour _____

_____

_____

Warranty _____

Cost _____

Budget _____

Variation _____

Scheduled Delivery Date _____

Delivery Date _____

Variation _____

Supplier _____

_____

Address _____

_____

Phone _____ Fax _____

Email _____

HANDY TIP

Dealing with Tradespeople and Others:
Always get a written quote detailing all of the work
and terms agreed to from anyone you will be hiring.
Be wary about paying a large amount up front.
Realistic progress payments are a better way to go.
Also, if you are not satisfied with any part of, or all
of the work, get the person who did it to rectify it
before paying anything. If you feel uncomfortable
or intimidated dealing with anyone involved in your
renovations or building project, ask a relative or
friend, particularly one who has some experience or
knowledge of home renovations or building, to be
present when you speak to them.

APPLIANCES – FITTINGS

RANGE HOOD

Type/Size/Brand/Colour _____

_____

_____

Warranty _____

Cost _____

Budget _____

Variation _____

Scheduled Delivery Date _____

Delivery Date _____

Variation _____

Supplier _____

_____

Address _____

_____

Phone _____ Fax _____

Email _____

HANDY TIP

Tradespeople: It is advisable to get several tradespeople to quote on each job. Whenever possible, use those who come recommended. It is a good idea to introduce yourself to the local hardware store or building material supplier staff and ask them if they can recommend any good reliable and reasonably priced tradesmen in the area. Also, ask any neighbours who have had recent work done or are in the process of doing renovations, if they can recommend those who they had engaged. When you find a good tradesperson, see if he or she can recommend other tradespeople.

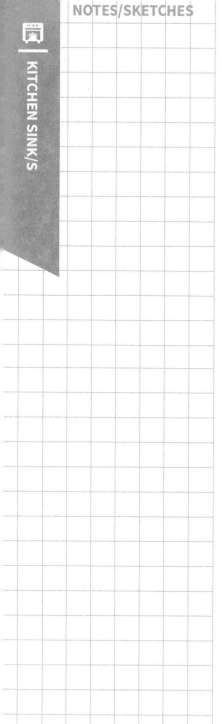

APPLIANCES – FITTINGS

KITCHEN

SINK/S

Type/Size/Brand/Colour/Quantity _____

_____

_____

_____

Warranty _____

Cost _____

Budget _____

Variation _____

Scheduled Delivery Date _____

Delivery Date _____

Variation _____

Supplier _____

_____

Address _____

_____

Phone _____ Fax _____

Email _____

HANDY TIP

Taking On A Number of Jobs: Some tradesmen start one job, then start another before finishing the first. Make sure those you engage commit to finishing your work from start to finish in the time they said they would. Check on their progress daily and even make a photographic record of it. Make sure all the tradespeople you use are licensed and covered by insurance.

APPLIANCES – FITTINGS

BATHROOM

SINK/S

Type/Size/Brand/Colour/Quantity _____

_____

_____

_____

Warranty _____

Cost _____

Budget _____

Variation _____

Scheduled Delivery Date _____

Delivery Date _____

Variation _____

Supplier _____

_____

Address _____

_____

Phone _____ Fax _____

Email _____

HANDY TIP

Recommendations: When speaking to a tradesperson, get the names and phone numbers of two previous customers who they have done work for and contact them and ask for their opinions on the work.

/ 63

APPLIANCES – FITTINGS

BATHROOM

BATH/S

Type/Size/Brand/Colour/Quantity _____

_____

_____

_____

Warranty _____

Cost _____

Budget _____

Variation _____

Scheduled Delivery Date _____

Delivery Date _____

Variation _____

Supplier _____

_____

Address _____

_____

Phone _____ Fax _____

Email _____

HANDY TIP

Choice of Intruders: One of the most common means of entry to premises by intruders is through windows. So, it is important to have installed the correct locks. Best get the experts to advise and install.

APPLIANCES – FITTINGS

BATHROOM

SHOWER BASE/S

Type/Size/Brand/Colour/Quantity _____

_____

_____

_____

Warranty _____

Cost _____

Budget _____

Variation _____

Scheduled Delivery Date _____

Delivery Date _____

Variation _____

Supplier _____

_____

Address _____

_____

Phone _____ Fax _____

Email _____

--- **HANDY TIP** ---

Take Photos: It would appear virtually everyone today has a cell phone. And all of these have a built-in camera. Therefore, take photos of areas or parts of the property which you will be working on, both inside and out. You can use them to show your hardware or paint expert what you are doing or planning. You can also keep them as a record of the work.

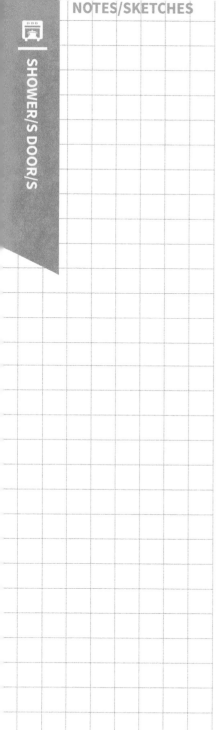

APPLIANCES – FITTINGS

SHOWER/S

DOOR/S

Type/Size/Brand/Colour/Quantity _____

_____

_____

_____

Warranty _____

Cost _____

Budget _____

Variation _____

Scheduled Delivery Date _____

Delivery Date _____

Variation _____

Supplier _____

_____

Address _____

_____

Phone _____ Fax _____

Email _____

HANDY TIP

Look After The Workers: If there is no place inside for workers to have their meal breaks and store their personal belongings, have them erect a temporary shelter out of tarpaulins. You can also supply seating such as in the form of simple plastic crates.

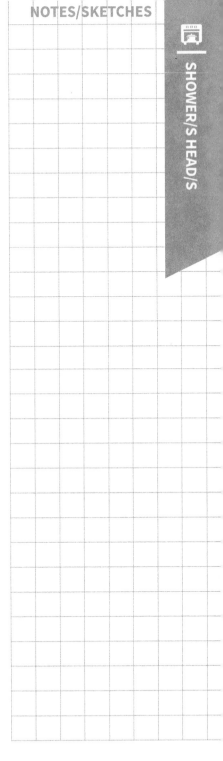

APPLIANCES – FITTINGS

SHOWER/S

HEAD/S

Type/Size/Brand/Colour/Quantity _____

_____

_____

_____

Warranty _____

Cost _____

Budget _____

Variation _____

Scheduled Delivery Date _____

Delivery Date _____

Variation _____

Supplier _____

_____

Address _____

_____

Phone _____ Fax _____

Email _____

HANDY TIP

Expect To Be Without Power/Water: Find
out in advance when electricians and plumbers
need to cut off supplies and plan accordingly.
There is no point in tradespeople turning up ready
to start work with electric tools and equipment,
just to find there is no power.

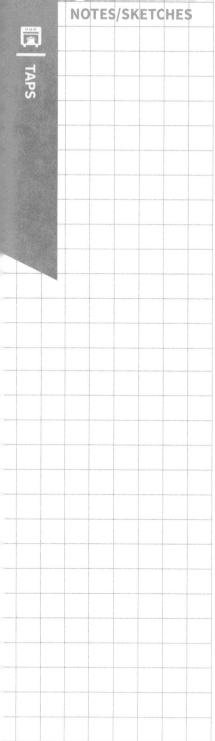

APPLIANCES – FITTINGS

TAPS

KITCHEN

Type/Size/Brand/Colour/Quantity _____

_____

Cost _____

Delivery Date _____

Supplier _____

Address _____

_____

Phone _____ Fax _____

Email _____

BATHROOM

Type/Size/Brand/Colour/Quantity _____

_____

Cost _____

Delivery Date _____

Supplier _____

Address _____

_____

Phone _____ Fax _____

Email _____

LAUNDRY

Type/Size/Brand/Colour/Quantity _____

_____

Cost _____

Delivery Date _____

Supplier _____

Address _____

_____

Phone _____ Fax _____

Email _____

APPLIANCES – FITTINGS

TOILET/S

CISTERN/S

Type/Size/Brand/Colour/Quantity _____

_____

Warranty _____

Cost _____

Budget _____

Variation _____

Scheduled Delivery Date _____

Delivery Date _____

Variation _____

Supplier _____

Address _____

_____

Phone _____ Fax _____

Email _____

SEAT/S

Type/Size/Brand/Colour/Quantity _____

_____

Cost _____

Budget _____

Variation _____

Scheduled Delivery Date _____

Delivery Date _____

Variation _____

Supplier _____

Address _____

_____

Phone _____ Fax _____

Email _____

CUPBOARDS – BENCHTOPS

KITCHEN CUPBOARDS/ BENCHTOPS

Types/Size/Brand/Colour/Quantity _____

_____

_____

_____

Warranty _____

Cost _____

Budget _____

Variation _____

Scheduled Delivery Date _____

Delivery Date _____

Variation _____

Supplier _____

_____

Address _____

_____

Phone _____ Fax _____

Email _____

HANDY TIP

Cover Up Furniture and Equipment: Often, all but very minor renovations can cause some dust or paint splatter. As well as being a possible health hazard, dust can also damage electronic equipment. So, use covers to protect furniture and equipment and put smaller decorative items such as framed photographs and ornaments in boxes or plastic bags while the work is being done.

BATHROOM CUPBOARDS/ VANITIES/BENCHTOPS

Types/Size/Brand/Colour/Quantity _____

_____

_____

_____

Warranty _____

Cost _____

Budget _____

Variation _____

Scheduled Delivery Date _____

Delivery Date _____

Variation _____

Supplier _____

_____

Address _____

_____

Phone _____ Fax _____

Email _____

BATHROOM CUPBOARDS/VANITIES/BENCHTOPS

HANDY TIP

Protect Yourself: If you have to demolish areas of the property before making improvements, make sure you wear the proper protections. It is important to wear good quality gloves when the job requires it. If there is going to be a lot of dust or small particles flying around, you should also wear eye protection and a mask. Sometimes hard hats are advisable.

/ 71

LAUNDRY CUPBOARDS/ BENCHTOPS

Types/Size/Brand/Colour/Quantity _____

_____

_____

_____

Warranty _____

Cost _____

Budget _____

Variation _____

Scheduled Delivery Date _____

Delivery Date _____

Variation _____

Supplier _____

_____

Address _____

_____

Phone _____ Fax _____

Email _____

HANDY TIP

Clear The Decks: A well known Naval phrase which goes back to the days of the great 'man-o-wars' of the Nelson era is 'Clear The Decks For Action'. The same should apply on renovation or building sites. Clutter and materials or equipment casually strewn around the floor or grounds are safety hazards. Have them stored out of the way.

LIGHTS

OUTSIDE

Types/Size/Brand/Colour/Quantity _____

_____

_____

_____

Cost _____

Budget _____

Variation _____

Scheduled Delivery Date _____

Delivery Date _____

Variation _____

Supplier _____

_____

Address _____

_____

Phone _____ Fax _____

Email _____

OUTSIDE LIGHTS

HANDY TIP

Plenty of Advice Available: There is no shortage of advice and information on renovations and home improvements available today. Bookstores and newsagents often have a large range of books and magazines dedicated solely to the subjects. The internet also has a great deal of information which you can source. So, whether you are planning tiling or landscaping, you can be sure there is some information available to help you.

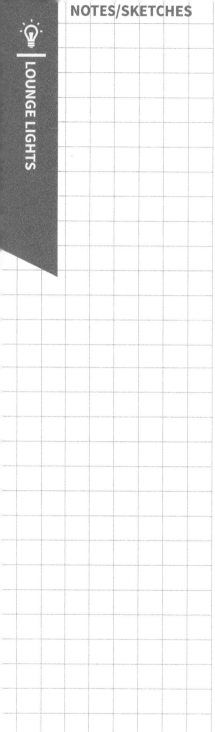

LIGHTS

LOUNGE

Types/Size/Brand/Colour/Quantity _____

_____

_____

_____

Cost _____

Budget _____

Variation _____

Scheduled Delivery Date _____

Delivery Date _____

Variation _____

Supplier _____

_____

Address _____

_____

Phone _____ Fax _____

Email _____

HANDY TIP

Budget: Most importantly – set a budget and use The Home Renovation Diary to keep a close check on it. Not all of the renovations have to be completed immediately. If your budget allows you to do only so much at a time then start with the essential work such as structural, waterproofing, security, electrical and plumbing/drainage. Then continue on with the kitchen, bathroom, toilet etc.

LIGHTS

BEDROOMS

Types/Size/Brand/Colour/Quantity _____

_____

_____

_____

Cost _____

Budget _____

Variation _____

Scheduled Delivery Date _____

Delivery Date _____

Variation _____

Supplier _____

_____

Address _____

_____

Phone _____ Fax _____

Email _____

HANDY TIP

Make Notes When Required: Use the
'Renovation Diary' or an extra notebook to record
details when required. These can range from
delivery dates to changes to design, installations
and construction.

BEDROOM LIGHTS

/ 75

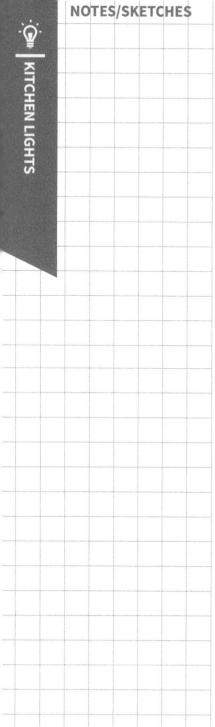

KITCHEN

Types/Size/Brand/Colour/Quantity _____

_____

_____

_____

Cost _____

Budget _____

Variation _____

Scheduled Delivery Date _____

Delivery Date _____

Variation _____

Supplier _____

_____

Address _____

_____

Phone _____ Fax _____

Email _____

— HANDY TIP —

Know Your Limitations: There are a great many jobs during renovations which can be done by almost anyone. Painting is one, providing you have the proper advice from your local paint supplier or hardware store. However, some jobs such as the obvious electric and plumbing work have to be done by professionals. Sure, have a go if you feel you can do the job, but don't tackle anything beyond your capabilities.

LIGHTS

LAUNDRY

Types/Size/Brand/Colour/Quantity _____

_____

_____

_____

Cost _____

Budget _____

Variation _____

Scheduled Delivery Date _____

Delivery Date _____

Variation _____

Supplier _____

_____

Address _____

_____

Phone _____ Fax _____

Email _____

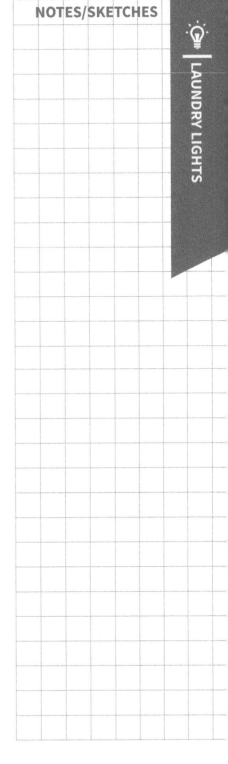

LAUNDRY LIGHTS

HANDY TIP

Be Wary of Electric Tools: The great range of electrical tools and equipment available to renovators and tradespeople today is wonderful and hasten considerably the completion of any job. However, they can also be dangerous – even lethal – if not used correctly and stored properly. Circular saws and all other types of saws, drills and the rest should always be handled with care. Also, be sure you don't touch electric connections with damp or wet hands. Water and electricity are a lethal combination.

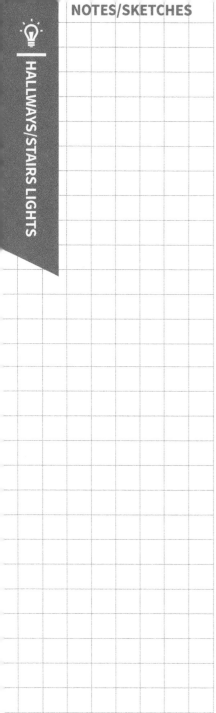

LIGHTS

HALLWAYS/STAIRS

Types/Size/Brand/Colour/Quantity _____

_____

_____

_____

Cost _____

Budget _____

Variation _____

Scheduled Delivery Date _____

Delivery Date _____

Variation _____

Supplier _____

_____

Address _____

_____

Phone _____ Fax _____

Email _____

HANDY TIP

Let There Be Light: Many older houses can be dark inside. However, there are a number of ways to lighten them up. One of the most obvious is by using light coloured, glossy paint on the walls and frames. Another is by 're-dressing' the windows by replacing dark coloured curtains and blinds or heavy dark stained louvers with lighter colours. A much more radical solution is to install one or more additional windows. That work will need to be done by professionals and possibly require council/local authority approval. Installing better lighting is another way of brightening up an area.

DOOR AND WINDOW HARDWARE

DOOR HANDLES

Types/Size/Brand/Quantity _____

_____

_____

_____

Cost _____

Budget _____

Variation _____

Scheduled Delivery Date _____

Delivery Date _____

Variation _____

Supplier _____

_____

Address _____

_____

Phone _____ Fax _____

Email _____

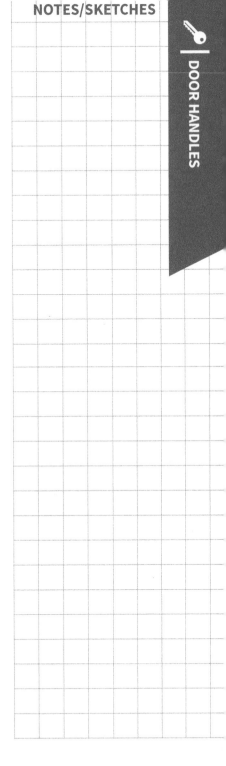

HANDY TIP

Fitting Door Handles: When purchasing door handles, select ones which will match the types you will be replacing. That way you will not have to drill new holes and fill old ones. If you choose correctly then they should just fit in. Take a sample or photograph and measurements to your local supplier and he or she will be able to help.

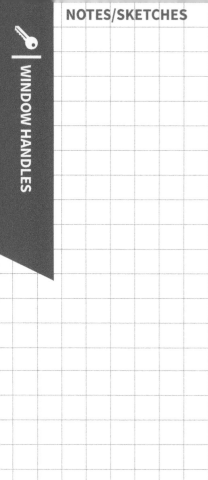

DOOR AND WINDOW HARDWARE

WINDOW HANDLES

Types/Size/Brand/Quantity _____

_____

_____

_____

Cost _____

Budget _____

Variation _____

Scheduled Delivery Date _____

Delivery Date _____

Variation _____

Supplier _____

_____

Address _____

_____

Phone _____ Fax _____

Email _____

———— HANDY TIP ————

Use Easy To Reach Handles: As with door handles, window handles come in a large variety of types and sizes. So, choose ones which are best suited to your needs. Consider what windows you might want to open frequently and get easy to operate and reach handles to fit to them.

DOOR AND WINDOW HARDWARE

DOOR LOCKS

Types/Size/Brand/Quantity _____

_____

_____

_____

Cost _____

Budget _____

Variation _____

Scheduled Delivery Date _____

Delivery Date _____

Variation _____

Supplier _____

_____

Address _____

_____

Phone _____ Fax _____

Email _____

HANDY TIP

Best To Install Good Quality: It is always
advisable to install good quality locks on all outside
doors. There are many types for you to choose from.
If you have a builder or carpenter, they can advise
you on the best type to purchase. You can also get
advice from your local locksmith's shop or hardware
store staffs.

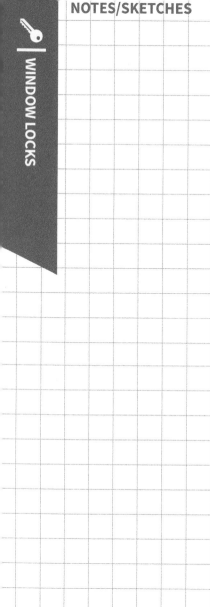

NOTES/SKETCHES

WINDOW LOCKS

WINDOW LOCKS

Types/Size/Brand/Quantity _____

_____

_____

_____

Cost _____

Budget _____

Variation _____

Scheduled Delivery Date _____

Delivery Date _____

Variation _____

Supplier _____

_____

Address _____

_____

Phone _____ Fax _____

Email _____

HANDY TIP

Choice of Intruders: One of the most common means of entry to premises by intruders is through windows. So, it is important to have installed the correct locks. Best get the experts to advise and install.

DOOR AND WINDOW HARDWARE

DOOR HINGES

Types/Size/Brand/Quantity _____

_____

_____

_____

Cost _____

Budget _____

Variation _____

Scheduled Delivery Date _____

Delivery Date _____

Variation _____

Supplier _____

_____

Address _____

_____

Phone _____ Fax _____

Email _____

HANDY TIP

Replacing Doors: One thing which lifts the appearance of any home is the front door, and there are many designs available to choose from. Also, bright new interior doors can make a big difference to the appeal of any home. Having them installed by a professional would not be a big job and should not cost a great deal. However, if you are handy, you might consider doing it yourself.

NOTES/SKETCHES

DOOR HINGES

DOOR AND WINDOW HARDWARE

WINDOW HINGES

Types/Size/Brand/Quantity _____

_____

_____

_____

Cost _____

Budget _____

Variation _____

Scheduled Delivery Date _____

Delivery Date _____

Variation _____

Supplier _____

_____

Address _____

_____

Phone _____ Fax _____

Email _____

HANDY TIP

Good Handymen Might Do: While good capable tradesmen will be needed for a great many jobs, often handymen will be able to do the work. And, they should charge quite a bit less. So, if the job does not require a qualified person, check around and see if you can find a good local handyman.

SECURITY SYSTEMS

Types/Number of Units/Brand _____

_____

_____

Warranty _____

Cost _____

Budget _____

Variation _____

Scheduled Delivery Date _____

Delivery Date _____

Variation _____

Supplier _____

_____

Address _____

_____

Phone _____ Fax _____

Email _____

HANDY TIP

Burglar Proof: It is a good idea to change all the locks on a property you buy. Even if they are in good working order, you can never tell for certain if there are any extra keys in existence. Also, upgrade or install security devices and take out insurance as soon as possible. It is a well known fact that burglars and vandals target unoccupied homes which are being renovated. They will steal almost anything, from tools and equipment to large appliances, even those still in their crates or cartons. Premises which are being renovated have also been vandalized and even set alight by intruders.

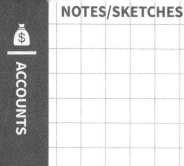

ACCOUNTS

DATE	JOB/ITEMS	COSTS

ACCOUNTS

DATE	JOB/ITEMS	COSTS

ACCOUNTS

/ 87

CPSIA information can be obtained
at www.ICGtesting.com
Printed in the USA
LVHW071449030120
642457LV00014B/967/P